SCHOLASTIC

News

Nonfiction Readers

A Home on the Tundra

By Katie Marsico

Children's Press®
A Division of Scholastic Inc.
New York Toronto London Auckland Sydney
Mexico City New Delhi Hong Kong
Danbury, Connecticut

These content vocabulary word builders are for grades 1–2.
Subject Consultant: Susan Woodward, Professor of Geography, Radford University, Radford, Virginia

Reading Consultant: Cecilia Minden-Cupp, PhD, Former Director of the Language and Literacy Program, Harvard Graduate School of Education, Cambridge, Massachusetts

Photographs © 2007: Alamy Images/Angelo Cavalli: 4 top, 8; Corbis Images: 5 top right, 12 (David Samuel Robbins), 1, 11 (Alison Wright); milosphotos.com/Milo Burcham: 5 bottom left, 16; Minden Pictures: 19, 20 bottom (Colin Monteath/Hedgehog House), 21 top (Cyril Ruoso/JH Editorial), back cover, cover center inset, 2, 4 bottom right, 5 bottom right, 7, 9, 17, 23 top left (Zhinong Xi); Nature Picture Library Ltd./Gertrud & Helmut Denzau: 23 bottom left; NHPA/Andy Rouse: 21 bottom; Photo Researchers, NY: cover right inset, 23 bottom right (W.K. Fletcher), 23 top right (Martin Harvey), 20 top (T. Kitchin/V. Hurst), cover left inset, 4 bottom left, 15 (Terry Whittaker); Ric Ergenbright: cover background, 5 top left, 13.

Book Design: Simonsays Design!
Book Production: The Design Lab

Library of Congress Cataloging-in-Publication Data

Marsico, Katie, 1980–
 A home on the tundra / by Katie Marsico.
   p. cm. — (Scholastic news nonfiction readers)
 Includes index.
 ISBN-10: 0-516-25345-X
 ISBN-13: 978-0-516-25345-9
 1. Tundra ecology—Juvenile literature. I. Title. II. Series.
 QH541.5.T8M37 2006
 577.5'3—dc22   2006002306

2 3 4 5 6 7 8 9 10 R 16 15 14 13 12 11 10 09 08

CONTENTS

WORD HUNT

Look for these words as you read. They will be in **bold**.

habitat
(**hab**-uh-tat)

snow leopard
(**sno leh**-purd)

tundra
(**tuhn**-druh)

4

lichens
(**lie**-kunz)

shrubs
(**shruhbz**)

woolly hares
(**wuh**-lee **hares**)

yaks
(**yaks**)

What Is This Place?

The wind is so cold you can hardly breathe. The rocky soil feels frozen.

You look around, but you don't see any trees. Suddenly, you hear a wolf howl.

Where are we?

When wolves howl, it is their way of talking to one another.

We're on the Asian **tundra**!

The tundra is a type of **habitat**. A habitat is where a plant or animal usually lives.

Few trees grow on the tundra, and temperatures are often freezing.

habitat

The tundra is the coldest habitat on the planet!

There are four seasons on the Asian tundra.

Spring, summer, and fall are cool and very short. Winter is freezing cold. It lasts a long, long time.

Winter is the longest
season on the tundra.

11

The tundra has few trees, but wildflowers and other plants grow there.

Short, woody plants called **shrubs** grow close to the ground. Moss and colorful **lichens** cover rocks.

shrubs

Lichens often grow on hard surfaces such as rocks.

How can animals, such as this **snow leopard**, stand the freezing temperatures? Over time, its body has changed in special ways to help it live on the tundra.

Snow leopards have thick fur on their feet. This keeps their feet warm when they walk.

Brown bears, gray wolves, and **yaks** are found on the tundra.

Wild sheep, deer, and **woolly hares** also live there. A woolly hare is a wild rabbit.

woolly hare

Yaks use their horns to dig under the snow for food.

The tundra is an exciting place to explore! Dress warm and head through the snow. You'll meet these blue sheep and other amazing animals that live in this habitat!

A DAY IN THE LIFE OF A SNOW LEOPARD

How does a snow leopard spend most of its time? When it is not hunting, a snow leopard sleeps in rocky areas such as caves.

What does a snow leopard eat? A snow leopard eats sheep, woolly hares, deer, and birds.

What are a snow leopard's enemies?
Humans are a snow leopard's enemies.

Does a snow leopard have a special survival trick?
A snow leopard blends in with its surroundings. The color of its spots and fur helps it hide in rocky areas.

YOUR NEW WORDS

habitat (**hab**-uh-tat) the place where a plant or animal usually lives

lichens (**lie**-kunz) plants that usually grow on a solid surface such as a rock

shrubs (**shruhbz**) short, woody plants that usually grow close to the ground

snow leopard (**sno leh**-purd) a large wildcat that lives in Central Asia and has thick, whitish fur

tundra (**tuhn**-druh) a treeless plain where temperatures are often freezing

woolly hares (**wuh**-lee **hares**) wild rabbits that live on the tundra

yaks (**yaks**) long-haired, cowlike animals

OTHER ANIMALS THAT LIVE ON THE TUNDRA

antelopes

cranes

marmots

pikas

INDEX

FIND OUT MORE

Book:

Cefrey, Holly. *Tundra.* New York: PowerKids Press, 2003.

Website:

MBGnet: Tundra Topics
http://mbgnet.mobot.org/sets/tundra/

MEET THE AUTHOR:

Katie Marsico works as a managing editor of children's reference books. She lives with her family not far from Chicago, Illinois, which she imagines gets just as windy and cold as the tundra!